Pet
Parrots
UP CLOSE

by Karon Dubke

Gail Saunders-Smith, PhD, Consulting Editor

CAPSTONE PRESS
a capstone imprint

Pebble Plus is published by Capstone Press,
1710 Roe Crest Drive, North Mankato, Minnesota 56003
www.capstonepub.com

Library of Congress Cataloging-in-Publication Data
Dubke, Karon, author.
Pet Parrots Up Close/by Karon Dubke.
pages cm.—(Pebble Plus. Pets Up Close)
Summary: "Full-color, zoomed-in photos and simple text describe pet parrots' body parts"—Provided by publisher.
Audience: Ages 5–8.
Audience: K to grade 3.
Includes bibliographical references and index.
ISBN 978-1-4914-0581-9 (hardcover)
ISBN 978-1-4914-0615-1 (ebook pdf)
1. Parrots—Juvenile literature. 2. Cage birds—Juvenile literature. I. Title.
QL696.P7D83 2015
636.6'865—dc23   2014012289

Editorial Credits
Jeni Wittrock, editor; Bobbie Nuytten, designer; Svetlana Zhurkin, media researcher; Katy LaVigne, production specialist

Photo Credits
Capstone Studio: Karon Dubke, cover, 1, 11, 15, 17, 21; Shutterstock: Eric Isselee, 9, Kuttelvaserova Stuchelova, 19, Mikael Damkier, 13, Panu Ruangjan, 7, Redchanka, 5

Note to Parents and Teachers

The Pets Up Close set supports national science standards related to life science. This book describes and illustrates pet parrots. The images support early readers in understanding the text. The repetition of words and phrases helps early readers learn new words. This book also introduces early readers to subject-specific vocabulary words, which are defined in the Glossary section. Early readers may need assistance to read some words and to use the Table of Contents, Glossary, Read More, Internet Sites, and Index sections of the book.

Printed in the United States of America in North Mankato, Minnesota
052014   008087CGF14

Table of Contents

Pet Parrots

Hello, pretty bird!

Who said that?

It's a pet bird called a parrot.

Let's take an up-close look at

these talkative, feathered friends.

Parrot Feathers

Birds are the only animals with feathers. Parrots fluff their feathers to warm up or cool down. A healthy parrot's feathers are clean and smooth.

Parrot Wings

Parrots have strong wings to fly away from danger. Pet parrots need roomy cages to stretch and flap their wings.

9

Parrot Tails

Parrots' feathered tails help them balance. Friendly parrots wag their tails when they're happy to see you. Never pull a parrot's tail. That hurts a lot!

11

Parrot Eyes

Parrots have eyes on
the sides of their heads.
They can watch for danger
all around them.

13

Parrot Ears

Have you ever seen a parrot's ear? Look carefully under its feathers. The feathers quiet the sound of the wind when parrots fly.

15

Parrot Noses

A parrot breathes through
two holes above its beak.
This spot is called a **cere**.
Male parakeets have blue ceres.
A female's cere is pink or tan.

say it like this: SEER

cere

Parrot Feet

Parrots' feet have two toes in front and two toes in back. Their toes are perfect for grabbing, climbing, and gripping branches.

Parrot Beaks

Parrots use their curved beaks like we use our fingers. Parrots eat, climb, and pick up treats with their beaks. What a good bird!

Huayangosaurus lived in the forests of what is now China.

where this dinosaur lived

HUAYANGOSAURUS' plates are more narrow and pointed than most stegosaurs.

HUAYANGOSAURUS used its spiked tail to protect itself. One swing from its tail could hurt hungry predators.

13

HUAYANGOSAURUS was one of the first plated dinosaurs. It lived 20 million years before Stegosaurus.

HUAYANGOSAURUS had 14 teeth in the front of its mouth. The dinosaur used its front teeth to eat tough plants, such as ferns and conifers.

KENTROSAURUS

PRONOUNCED: KEN-tro-SAWR-us

NAME MEANING: pointed lizard

TIME PERIOD LIVED: Late Jurassic Period, about 150 million years ago

LENGTH: 15 feet (4.5 m)

WEIGHT: 1.1 tons (1 metric ton)

TYPE OF EATER: herbivore

PHYSICAL FEATURES: two rows of pointed plates down its neck and back, sharp spikes on shoulders and tail

KENTROSAURUS' tail was longer than the rest of its body.

Kentrosaurus lived in swamps in what is now Tanzania.

N
W E
S

■ where this dinosaur lived

KENTROSAURUS had a very good sense of smell.

Many **KENTROSAURUS** fossils were destroyed by bombs during Word War II (1939-1945).

LEXOVISAURUS

PRONOUNCED: lek-SOH-vi-SAWR-us

NAME MEANING: Lexovii lizard, after an ancient Celtic tribe in France

TIME PERIOD LIVED: Middle Jurassic Period, about 165 million years ago

LENGTH: 20 feet (6 m)

WEIGHT: 2.6 tons (2.4 metric tons)

TYPE OF EATER: herbivore

PHYSICAL FEATURES: two rows of plates on its back, spikes along its tail

LEXOVISAURUS fossils are displayed at the National Museum of Natural History in Paris, France.

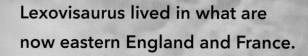

Lexovisaurus lived in what are now eastern England and France.

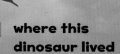

where this dinosaur lived

STEGOSAURUS

PRONOUNCED: STEG-uh-SAWR-us

NAME MEANING: plated lizard

TIME PERIOD LIVED: Late Jurassic Period, about 150 million years ago

LENGTH: 25 feet (8 m)

WEIGHT: 3.4 tons (3.1 metric tons)

TYPE OF EATER: herbivore

PHYSICAL FEATURES: bony plates on its back, sharp spikes on its tail

STEGOSAURUS was the largest plated dinosaur. It had larger spikes than other plated dinosaurs.

Stegosaurus lived in the forests and swamps of North America.

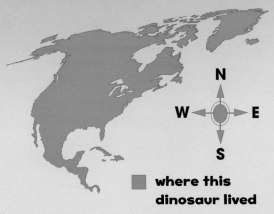

N
W ← ⊙ → E
S

■ where this dinosaur lived

Fossils show **STEGOSAURUS** fought the predator Allosaurus. Some Allosaurus fossils have holes from Stegosaurus spikes. Some Stegosaurus plates have been found with Allosaurus bite marks.

STEGOSAURUS tore leaves off plants with its bony beak. It chewed the leaves with its back teeth.

The first **STEGOSAURUS** fossil was discovered in Colorado in 1876.

STEGOSAURUS traveled in herds. This may have protected the dinosaur from predators.

STEGOSAURUS' plates were made out of keratin.

TUOJIANGOSAURUS

PRONOUNCED: TOO-oh-GEE-an-GO-SAWR-us

NAME MEANING: Tuo River lizard

TIME PERIOD LIVED: Late Jurassic Period, about 160 million years ago

LENGTH: 22 feet (6.7 m)

WEIGHT: 3.1 tons (2.8 metric tons)

TYPE OF EATER: herbivore

PHYSICAL FEATURES: plates on its back, spikes on its tail

TUOJIANGOSAURUS looked similar to Stegosaurus. Both dinosaurs had flat, thick plates.

Tuojiangosaurus lived in the
forests of what is now China.

where this
dinosaur lived

N
W · E
S

TUOJIANGOSAURUS was prey
for the fearsome predator
Yangchuanosaurus.

TUOJIANGOSAURUS was named 100 years after Stegosaurus.

TUOJIANGOSAURUS had a tiny brain compared to its body.

TUOJIANGOSAURUS had
17 pairs of plates and spikes.

YINGSHANOSAURUS

PRONOUNCED: ying-SHAN-uh-SAW-rus

NAME MEANING: Golden Hills reptile, fossils were discovered in Yingshan, China

TIME PERIOD LIVED: Late Jurassic Period, about 155 million years ago

LENGTH: 13 to 16 feet (4 to 5 m)

WEIGHT: 1.6 tons (1.5 metric tons)

TYPE OF EATER: herbivore

PHYSICAL FEATURES: long shoulder spikes that looked like wings

Paleontologists do not know a lot about this dinosaur. Only one **YINGSHANOSAURUS** skeleton has been discovered. But it is missing.

Yingshanosaurus lived in the forests of what is now China.

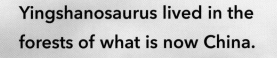

where this dinosaur lived

N
W — E
S

YINGSHANOSAURUS may have traveled in herds.

YINGSHANOSAURUS has a similar name to another dinosaur called Yangchuanosaurus. But the two dinosaurs were very different. Yangchuanosaurus was a meat-eater that walked on two legs.

GLOSSARY

BEAK (BEEK)—the hard, pointed part of an animal's mouth

CONIFER (KON-uh-fur)—a tree with cones and narrow leaves called needles

FERN (FUHRN)—a plant with feathery leaves and no flowers; ferns usually grow in damp places

FOSSIL (FOSS-uhl)—the remains of an animal or plant from millions of years ago that have turned to rock

HERBIVORE (HUR-buh-vor)—an animal that eats only plants

HERD (HURD)—a group of the same kind of animals that live and travel together

JURASSIC PERIOD (ju-RASS-ik PIHR-ee-uhd)—the second period of the Mesozoic Era; the Jurassic Period was from 200 to 145 million years ago

KERATIN (KAIR-uh-tin)—the hard substance that forms a person's fingernails and toenails

PALEONTOLOGIST (pale-ee-uhn-TOL-uh-jist)—a scientist who studies fossils

PLATE (PLAYT)—a flat, bony growth

PRAIRIE (PRAIR-ee)—a large area of flat grassland

PREDATOR (PRED-uh-tur)—an animal that hunts other animals for food

PRONOUNCE (proh-NOUNSS)—to say a word in a certain way

SPIKE (SPIKE)—a sharp, pointy object; some dinosaurs used spikes to defend themselves

SWAMP (SWAHMP)—an area of wet, spongy ground

THAGOMIZER (THA-goh-MYE-zur)—the tail of a stegosaur dinosaur that has four to ten spikes

WORLD WAR II—a war in which the United States, France, Great Britain, the Soviet Union, and other countries defeated Germany, Italy, and Japan; World War II lasted from 1939 to 1945

CRITICAL THINKING USING THE COMMON CORE

1. How did Gigantspinosaurus get its name? Use the text to help you with your answer. (Key Ideas and Details)

2. Dinosaurs such as Hesperosaurus have thagomizers at the ends of their tails. What is a thagomizer? (Craft and Structure)

3. Yingshanosaurus and Yangchuanosaurus have similar names. How are these dinosaurs different? (Key Ideas and Details)

READ MORE

Silverman, Buffy. *Can You Tell a Stegosaurus from an Ankylosaurus?* Dinosaur Look-Alikes. Minneapolis: Lerner Publications Company, 2014.

Wegwerth, A.L. *Stegosaurus.* Little Paleontologist. North Mankato, Minn.: Capstone Press, 2015.

Woodward, John. *Everything You Need to Know about Dinosaurs: and Other Prehistoric Creatures.* New York: DK Publishing, 2014.

INTERNET SITES

FactHound offers a safe, fun way to find Internet sites related to this book. All of the sites on FactHound have been researched by our staff.

Here's all you do:

Visit *www.facthound.com*

Type in this code: 9781491496480

Super-cool stuff!

Check out projects, games and lots more at
www.capstonekids.com

INDEX